Breaking Family Ties

By Michelle D. Cook-Hall

Breaking Family Ties

Copyright © 2016. All rights reserved.

No part of this publication may be reproduced, stored in a retrieval system or transmitted in any way by any means, electronic, mechanical, photocopy, recording or otherwise, without the prior permission of the author except as provided by USA copyright law.

All characters appearing in this work are fictitious. Any resemblance to real persons, living or dead, is purely coincidental.

The opinions expressed by the author are not necessarily those of Revival Waves of Glory Books & Publishing.

Published by Revival Waves of Glory Books & Publishing

PO Box 596 | Litchfield, Illinois 62056 USA

www.revivalwavesofgloryministries.com

Revival Waves of Glory Books & Publishing is committed to excellence in the publishing industry.

Book design Copyright © 2016 by Revival Waves of Glory Books & Publishing. All rights reserved.

Published in the United States of America

Paperback: 978-1-68411-045-2

Table of Contents

Introduction 5
About The Author 7
Dedication 9

Chapter 1:
Pre-Exposed 11

Chapter 2:
Generational Curses 19

Chapter 3:
Broken Promises 29

Chapter 4:
Legal Rights 35

Chapter 5:
Renewing Your Mind 47

Chapter 6:
Complacency Is a Curse 55

Chapter 7:
Proclamation 61

Chapter 8:
Purpose Filled Life 65

Chapter 9:
The Buck Stops Here 69

Chapter 10:
Freedom 79

Breaking Family Ties

Michelle D. Cook-Hall

Introduction

As I enter the doctor's office, I am overwhelmed. Immediately I am handed paperwork with a list of physical and mental diseases. I am advised to review these forms and note if I or a family member has ever been diagnosed with any of the listed diseases. When I was in my youth, I would just check no to the questions without giving it a second thought. But as I approach adult hood, and have personally witnessed the demise of family members due to these listed diseases, I found myself studying the list. Not only was I studying the list of diseases, but fear began to set in when I realize that according to my doctor, I was pre-exposed to these diseases. I mean really how many times have a medical professional diagnosed someone with an ailment, only to say that it's hereditary. So what my ears hear and has warned my consciousness is that no matter what I do, I'm stuck with some disease because of my family's D.N.A. What a real crush and blow to my future. As unbelievable as it all seems, I realize that it was definitely authentic.

This process goes against everything that I was taught and believe. I just believed that despite what my family's curse was, it did not have to be my future. No matter what disease, sickness, or cycle my family embraced or displayed, I did not have to accept it as my own.

After watching family members suffer from hypertension, cancer, diabetes, depression, anxiety, asthma, heart conditions, schizophrenia, and mood swings, I decided that the buck stops here. It's time to embrace a new and brighter future. It is time to "Break the Family Ties". That's right! I will not embrace pre-mature death. I will not follow patterns of self-destruction by speaking failure into my life. I will dare to think out of the box. I will attempt to do something unlike the pattern set before me. I will think and speak life, health, strength, and prosperity over my mind, body, soul, and spirit. Not only that but I will train and teach my children to also press beyond the pattern and dare to be different. The place is here; the time is now to "Break the Family Ties".

About The Author

Michelle was born a Preacher's Kid to Edward and Sadie Cook. In her youth, Michelle served as Director of the Youth Choir and eventually served as Minister of Music. As a teenager, she founded the Prayer Warriors Church Drama Club providing opportunities of expression and faith. Having the heart of servitude, she organized clothes drives for Homeless Women Shelters and those in need. She wrote letters of encouragement and empowerment to those incarcerated in women's prison. While in College, she briefly worked as a writer for Urban Ministries Young Adult Sunday School books.

She graduated in 1997 with a Bachelor's of Science Degree. Following one accomplishment after another, she married her best friend, Mr. Ricky Hall, and they are now the proud parents of Jeremy, Brandon, and Jessica Hall. She served eight years as Business Manager and Grant Writer for Prayer Warriors Church, before beginning her career as a Human Service Caseworker for the State of Illinois.

She received her license to the Ministry in October of 2006, and immediately walking into her destiny by serving as Praise and Worship leader at Prayer Warriors Church in Chicago, IL. She has also hosted several annual Conferences such as Heart of Worship Conference and Power Weekend Conference. These Conferences are designed to empower and equip people to walk in their destiny and pursue their purpose. Michelle published her first book in 2013 entitled This Journey is a Process. This book inspired many to persevere and be strong. Motivated by her daughter, she released Mimi's Children Book Series with two books listed Mimi's Secret, and The Bully. She is so grateful for the opportunity to be able to share with the world her voice, her vision, her passion in words.

Michelle D. Cook-Hall

Dedication

This book is dedicated to my dearly departed sister Yolanda Cook. Yolanda struggle her entire life with health issues but yet was one of the strongest people I have ever known. I watched her struggle to be strong with a weak body, and it broke my heart. She was my biggest fan and cheerleader. I miss our long talks and sharing our journey together. I will always love and adore my sister "Makidada".

A special thanks to my husband Ricky and children, Jeremy, Brandon, and Jessica. Thank you for allowing me to put myself in my work and encourage me all the way. You guys are my motivation to share this message of love, hope, and power.

Although my father Edward W. Cook is no longer here in the flesh, I still fill his love and guidance to keep moving forward and fulfill my purpose. And finally to my mother Sadie Cook, you have taught me some much. You are a living, breathing, walking and talking encyclopedia. I remember sitting under your teaching in my youth. I would absorb every word from your mouth, completely mesmerize. You are such an inspiration to all and role model to many.

Please know that your life is meaningful and rich. My life is better because of your teaching and guidance.

Chapter 1:
Pre-Exposed

There is nothing more beautiful than a glowing pregnant woman. People are often drawn to a pregnant woman excited about the amazing journey of creation. Questions are often thrown at her like: When is your baby do? How do you feel? Are you excited? You never hear questions like: What diseases is your baby pre-exposed to? Are you afraid that your baby may inherit your Mom's mood swings or your father's anger? No, you never hear these questions proposed to a new mother. And that's because it is not polite to dig into someone else's family history and taint a celebratory moment. But truth be told, it's definitely something that should be discussed and researched. A parent should be aware of the genetics and behavior of the family tree.

Parents play music and sing to their unborn child, hoping to bring comfort and culture to their child. Some parents even expose their unborn child to foreign languages, math, and other educational resources to begin the process of stimulating their intelligence. Even the setting for the birth of the child is considerate. Parents choose natural settings over sterile hospitals, hoping to create a peaceful entry for the baby. Parents choose water births to ease a child into the new environment. But what about the parents who do the total opposite of what we just described. The parents who were not prepared for the child and is not excited. Maybe they are in a bad relationship, and the pending child is a reminder of their current dilemma. The parent who constantly tell everybody that they don't want a baby, and that they had no plans of parenthood. The self-destructive parent that smokes, drinks and party excessively while carrying the baby. If we believe that all of the positive activities and habits parents perform while carrying a baby will benefit the baby, then we must also believe that all of the negative activities and habits parents perform will also affect the baby in the womb.

The connection between an unborn baby and mother is simply amazing. There is not enough research in the world to clearly describe the experience. A pregnant woman can eat certain foods, and the unborn baby will respond either positively or negatively. A pregnant woman can crave foods that under any normal circumstances she would never have eaten. For example, I am allergic to certain fruits including watermelon, but while I was pregnant, I was able to eat all fruit including watermelon without any reaction. I carried oranges and plums in my bag everywhere I went because the craving for fruit was very strong. People applauded my healthy choices, but I often just chuckled because it was not my choices, I would've chosen a burger for myself. The needs of my unborn baby superseded my selfish desires.

An unborn child also responds to the emotional state of the mother. If a mother is stressed and emotional, this will also cause the unborn baby to feel stressed putting the unborn baby at risk. So it is safe to say that even in the womb, we are sponges and are being prepared for our journey out of the womb. I know of several mothers who while carrying their baby were stressed, sad, cried a lot and completely miserable for different reasons. When they gave birth, their baby had physical issues varying from heart conditions, delayed growth, underdeveloped organs etc. I'm not saying that all depress or emotionally stressed pregnant women will experience similar conditions with their unborn children, but I am saying that there is an existing risk due to the connection of mom and unborn child.

When a baby is born, the baby is already familiar with the voices that he heard from the womb. There are even stories of babies refusing to leave the side of their mother right after delivery by crying intensively until they are returned to the mother. An unborn baby has shared a body with the mother for 9 months. They have laughed together, cried together, and even gotten sick together creating the connection. I remember when I was pregnant with my second son. I had a severe case of claustrophobia. I couldn't even sit in the back seat of a car, because I felt as if I was being suffocated. I had never a feeling like this before, even with my first child. Well one day during a normal ultra sound, I saw the technician face change as she ran to contact the doctor. Now her response made me extremely concern. I attempted to question her about what she saw, but of course, she wouldn't discuss anything without the doctor. It turns out that my son had very little amniotic fluid. It was so low that my doctor just knew that he would come out with some form of health issues or deformities. He was being smashed and very uncomfortable in the womb. As a mom, immediately I knew that what I was feeling was directly related to what my unborn son was feeling in the womb.

We all love a happy baby. We've all seen that little bundle of joy showing their gums to the whole world as if they had a mouth full of teeth. They bounce and jump at just the presence of their parents. I remember calling my youngest son Tigger, because he loved to bounce up and down and as soon as his little feet hit the ground he was jumping. It was the cutest thing I had ever seen. He didn't need a bouncer; he was his own bouncer. We've all seen the adventurous baby that loves to explore and has to be watch with a close eye. The one that loves to zoom past mom and dad just for the adventure. My oldest son was famous for climbing up on counters and then calling for me to come and "Help". He did this faithfully, even while visiting my parent's home. As parents, we try to encourage our little ones to be independent but yet know we are always there to help.

I think one of the first things I noticed as a new mom was that as I was nurturing and training my little one to be healthy and strong, there were parents doing the total opposite. I've seen parents use foul language toward their baby, yell at the baby and even neglect the needs of the baby. Today I've seen videos and pictures on social media of parents smoking drugs in the face of their children, giving their children cigarettes and alcohol to drink and even encouraging their children to use foul language as if it is cute and acceptable behavior. I almost fell out of my seat watching adults instigate small children to fight as if they were animals. I remember a mother who kept cussing at her toddler in my presence, directing them to sit down and shut up. I was so frustrated with her behavior that I finally asked her to stop speaking to the baby that way. She began to tell me that the baby who was no more than 3 years old was a bad baby. Wow, I couldn't believe what this mother was saying, and I quickly explained to her that her behavior towards her baby was triggering her baby's behavior in response. In other words, she has learned to adapt to you and how to survive with you as her mom. She feels your aggression which is making her aggressive.

According to the Merriam-Webster, pre-exposed is to expose in advance or prematurely. In advance and prematurely, we are exposed to physical, mental, emotional and social defects. In contrast, we are also pre-exposed to healthy behavior and lifestyle. If a child is told Monday thru Friday that they are stupid and ugly, but on the weekend they are told they told they are smart and beautiful which descriptions will they believe? Well, I believe that what you hear the most takes precedence over anything else. In order for the brain to process information, it must first be stored.

So whenever a word is spoken it is stored in the brain. Recall is triggered by a retrieval cue, an environmental stimulus that prompts the brain to retrieve the memory. So this explains how when a baby hears the mother voice for the first time outside of the womb, they respond. Rather it was the comforting voice or just a familiar voice; the baby recalls the voice.

Parents are the first teachers of a child. A child is warned and advised early about what is safe and unsafe, what is good and what is bad. I think that unfortunately, adults underestimate the power of this process. Often times we just pass on behavior that our parents passed to us. "Do it, because I said so" is a phrase often used in the home during the development process. No explanations, just fear and punishment for failure to follow directions. It is not necessarily what parents say, but what they do that babies mimic.

I've watched my daughter actually stare at me while I'm brushing my teeth, only to mimic my every move as she brushes her teeth. If I spoke with a certain tone, I soon saw my daughter speaking with the same tone. She was literally following in my footsteps. I often joked and called her my shadow, because everywhere I go she is right behind me. The accountability to the healthy development of my daughter was my priority. She didn't just single out my positive characteristics; she embraced all of me. What it took me 41 years to create and breed it only took her 10 years to perfect. This further proves how perceptive children are and therefore it is our responsibility to monitor what they are exposed to.

Breaking Family Ties

Chapter 2:
Generational Curses

According to Lamentations 5:7 (NIV), *our ancestors sinned and are no more, and we bear their punishment.*

Generational Curses are described as a spiritual bondage that is passed down from one generation to another. One symptom of a generational curse is a continual negative pattern of something being handed down from generation to generation. For example, a father who is an alcoholic and verbally abuses his family, his son grows up and like father like son abuses alcohol and is abusive to his own family. Anger is so potent that even a child could display in the early stages of life. A child seen hitting and punching has been overlooked as just the child throwing a tantrum or bad parenting, but this could be a sign of anger. I remember speaking with a young mother and her son who was 4 years old. The little boy repeatedly hit her in the head and face as we attempted to converse. I finally got tired of watching the abuse and asked her why does he hit her like that and she laughed and stated she didn't know why he hit her. I assumed her laughter was from being embarrassed and not because she thought it was acceptable. The little boy looked at me and blurted out "My daddy, I get it from my daddy". I was speechless I couldn't believe that this boy solved this mystery in the presence of his mom. I looked at her and said well now you know. If only she would have spoken with her son, instead of just breeding and feeding his bad behavior she would have known that he was following the pattern of his father.

Growing up, my family was known to yell in the house. Even if we are having a good time and talking to each other, we were known for speaking extremely loudly. We are very passionate people, with very strong opinions. So when we all came together, the volume was on high as we attempted to out talk each other. As if speaking loudly would better get our point across, our kitchen was filled with high-pitched voices and hands held high. I never thought this was an issue, until I brought my future husband around who exposed me to the truth. He could not believe how my family communicated. He was literally shocked by the way we would sit around the table and just scream and yell discussing topics. Now this might seem harmless to you, but believe it or not, it has truly impacted my life. When I finally had my own family, I continued the cycle of yelling to get my point across. It's was as if I was watching myself, knowing that I should retreat but just continued.

Over the years I saw this for what it was, abuse. I was using my mouth as a weapon. I was manipulating and controlling with my high volume rants. This was a learned and practiced behavior. For example, every morning when my father awoke, he would yell upstairs to wake us up. He didn't see anything wrong with it, but it drove us crazy. But we dare not complain about this behavior because we were raised in the do as I say not as I do era.

The stress was so visible in my household. My father was a Pastor of a Baptist Church, and he had many responsibilities and demands. His stress level was at a red alert every day. You could see his struggle as he worked nights as a University Police Officer and Pastor in the day. Due to his high-stress level, work ethic, and lack of sleep, my father suffered a stroke at 44 years old. That's right at 44 years old, my father a strong and dedicated father and husband collapse in his own front yard. He was so strong, but life had struck him down. Ten years later at the age of 54, he passed away from pneumonia. Now the reason I am sharing this family tragedy is to stress the age and conditions of my father's untimely death. There is nowhere in medical science that it is normal or acceptable for a 44 year old to have a stroke. I want to point out certain factors regarding my father's inherited health conditions. My father was diabetic, and suffered from hypertension and stress. These are all inherited conditions. In my father's eyes, I could see his desire to be well again, but the struggle between his desire and will was overwhelming. If you are constantly being told that your ailment is inherited, it's as if your mind just becomes overwhelmed with the thought that it has to be this way. Think about it, if you are sitting in your doctor's office and your condition is constantly deteriorating and your doctor's response is "Unfortunately this is an inherited disease that you are battling," how would that make you feel? Will you feel helpless and vulnerable? Well, I remember when a doctor told me that sometimes you can make all the right choices but still struggle with hereditary diseases due to your family traits. I'm sorry, but that was the worst information I ever received. I was determined to research this further to take control of my own life and health.

One of the first steps to dealing with generational curses is getting to the root. Recognize it is as curse and not necessarily something that you have to adopt or embrace. Get to the root, go down your family tree if you have to and do your research. Think about when you first experience your symptoms and what was going at that particular time in your life.

For example, for several years I had been dealing with respiratory and gastric ailments. At the age of 40 years old, I was diagnosed with asthma. Can you believe that? I've gone through my entire life with no asthma treatment, but suddenly I was struggling with this crippling disease. Not only that, but I was constantly in pain traveling back and forth to my doctor's office and emergency rooms because of GERD. Gastroesophageal Reflux Disease hit me with vengeance, and I truly wasn't ready. I tried every remedy and prescription I could, with no resolution. And the entire experience was draining. I was working full time, a mom, wife and serving in ministry, I had no time to have this crippling curse. So I remembered a conversation that I had with my sister once about her health. My sister had always struggled with health issues but one day I noticed that she was getting weaker and sicker before my very eyes. One day as we sat across from each other at lunch, I simply asked her "Yolanda what happened to you, how did your condition get progressively worse?" She looked at me and told me that when our father died, she began to deteriorate. She said that she just found it difficult to be mobile and breathe. So now instead of inhaler pumps, she now required oxygen tanks not just at night, but now everywhere she went. I watched my sister go from a slightly independent young woman to a dependent young woman due to her body resistance. Now going back to my conditions, I began to propose the same question to myself that I did to my sister. I asked myself, "Michelle when did all these issues transpire, what is the root?"

So I began my own investigation, and the subject was me. I thought about the stress that I had been suffering through and my first symptom from stress was hypertension. But I had to narrow it down to when I had my first experience with these crippling issues. I remember my sister was getting worse, and I was getting calls that she was in the hospital or she was too sick to come out of the house. I remember talking to my sister and telling her how ill I was feeling, and she said it was as if we were sharing symptoms.

I had moments when I was struggling to breathe, and I would call her, and she said she was having a really bad day with her breathing. If I was dizzy and felt as if I could faint, I would call her and she would say that she felt the same.

I remember one night while I was sleeping, I had this overwhelming feeling of dread. I was crying and weeping so hard in my sleep I could barely catch my breath. It was the most terrifying moment in my life, and I knew something was about to completely change my life. Well two weeks later, my phone rang at 5:00 am and it was my oldest brother, telling me rush to my parent's home. I remember him saying "You need to get to the house immediately, it's Yolanda." My dear sister passed away that day in my parent's home. That was the dreadful feeling that I had two weeks prior. My life had been changed and altered by the passing of my sister. So that was it, I had watched her become extremely ill and it was affecting me. And her death just about took me out. I could now see the root of my issues. It was now as clear as day. My family had been plagued with sickness in our youth and it just manifested in our adulthood. My father had passed away at 54 after having a stroke at 44 years old; my sister passed away at 48 years old after suffering from complications due to Pulmonary Hypertension. My parents and siblings suffer from respiratory, hypertension, heart conditions and anxiety. I literally mean everyone in the household has or is dealing with one or more of these symptoms. This could not be a coincidence. We have to address this and resolve it for ourselves and our children.

We have looked at physical and emotional curses now let's look at social and economic curses. Even in social and economic settings, you can see the effects of generational curses. Yes, I am saying that poverty can be a generational curse. How many times have you heard someone say that they will break the cycle and be different than those before them? I have seen a very disturbing cycle in which four generations with lack of educational experience, failure to own any property, and only income received is through government assistance programs. Now we are talking about both intentional and unintentional lack of drive and means to break the poverty cycle.

The cycle of poverty according to Wikipedia is defined as a phenomenon where poor families become impoverished for at least three generations. Another theory for the perpetual cycle of poverty is that poor people have their own culture with a different set of values and beliefs that keep them trapped within that cycle from generation to generation. Let me further explain, a young girl who is raised in an unsupervised home where it is acceptable and necessary to be an adult before her time. Her environment is her norm. So when she becomes a teenager, she is educated quickly by those in her environment who has previously made the same choices. Although she may not want this for her life or future, she is pressed on every side to put aside all of her dreams and plans and "do what she has to do." Years later she finds herself in the same predicament as her mother, grandmother, and great-grandmother before her. I knew of a 16 year old who had 2 children, after further conversation, I learned that her other 2 sisters had also had children in their teens. I've seen girls cry because they have nowhere to live, jumping from one house to the next with no support. They feel as if there is no life beyond what their current situation provides. The pull of hopelessness is so strong that I've see a pattern of drug and alcohol abuse in these cases. With a parent that is suffering from addictions and mental and emotional turmoil, the child also suffers. The child displays behavioral problems and does not perform well in school. I've seen a case where the mother suffered with anger and mood swings due to alcohol abuse and her child was so unruly in school; she had to sit in the class every day just to monitor the child. In this case, the entire family needed therapy. Her family background was filled with abuse and alcoholism and therefore that's all she ever knew.

The viciousness of this cycle is limitless and ruthless. It's not gender bias either. Young men, who are healthy and strong, fail to see their true potential. They are caught in a vicious mind numbing cycle of "living for the moment" and not planning but yet even considering their future. When a person fails to see their future, they become a person engulfed in death. Everything about that person becomes deadly. They almost become addicted to the idea of death. That's why a lot of murderers, especially young murderers have been known to play video games filled with death. They listen to music and watch movies with a death theme. They are fascinated with guns and violence. They're always looking over their shoulders with eyes always shifting to cover the perimeter because death is always around the corner. The mentality of I will do unto you, before you are able to do me.

The second step to dealing with generational curses is the ability to break the curse. Treat the cause not the symptoms to get to the root of the issue. Get to the primary source, the origin of the issues. John 8:36 (NIV) states: So if the Son sets you free, you will be free indeed. This is not a scripture to read and put to the side, but this is an anthem of freedom. It is so important to completely grasp the concept of freedom. Later we will discuss the true meaning of renewing your mind, because we must have a renewed mind in order to accept our true freedom and its benefits. Treating the cause can be a difficult process, because it takes you to a place that you have been avoiding or even been in denial about.

I know this young woman, who was raised in a household filled with drugs and abandonment. The parents were not there physically or emotionally during some of the most pertinent years of her life. Although on the outside she appear to have a very healthy and successful lifestyle, truth is she has no relationship with her parents because of her anger toward them both. She immediately dislikes anyone who even reminds her of her mother. This was not something that she even noticed that she was doing until I brought it to her attention. She's very angry and often vents about her childhood and how she could have been in a better place if not for her parents. Even as an adult she is still venting and hurting because of her parents. The residue of her childhood has completely affected her life as an adult. But instead of dealing with the root, she has chosen to deal with the symptoms. This has cause a lot of serious and unhealthy moments in her life. As we continued to speak over time she slowly began to deal with the root after years of resistance. She truly believed that her past had nothing to do with her present conditions. The resistance was so strong, that I began to understand the term "strong hold". She was being dominated by her past hurt, rejection and pain. It's important not only to recognize the root and truly understand it, but began the process of loosening the resistance. I call this a process, because some roots are more deeply rooted then others.

Chapter 3:
Broken Promises

When a child is born into this world, there is an unspoken promise automatically expected. It's expected from society and the child. As a newborn opens his eyes and looks upon the first adult he gazes on, he has an expectation. He expects someone to care, nurture, feed, and provide his needs until he is able to verbalize what his needs are. When he realizes that his only way of communication is not getting him what he needs, it will affect him physically and emotionally. Researchers have found babies whose cries are usually ignored will not develop healthy intellectual and social skills according to (*Leiberman, A. F., & Zeanah, H., Disorders of Attachment in Infancy, Infant Psychiatry 1995, 4:571-587*). Dr. Rao and colleagues at the National Institutes of Health showed that infants with prolonged crying (but not due to colic) in the first 3 months of life had an average IQ 9 points lower at 5 years of age. They also showed poor fine motor development according to (*M R Rao, et al; Long Term Cognitive Development in Children with Prolonged Crying, National Institutes of Health, Archives of Disease in Childhood 2004; 89:989-992*).

If we start life with broken promises, then we mostly likely will expect nothing but empty, broken promises. It's nothing worst then promising something to a child, and not only break your promise but be nonchalant about it. Kids are so innocent and in their mind, you are truly innocent until you prove yourself to be guilty. They learn really quickly who they can trust and who they cannot trust. Even then, they want to believe, so they still extend their hand of trust giving you the benefit of the doubt. I remember speaking with a young child who was dealing with stress because of their parent's behavior. And innocently she said, "I'm only a kid, I shouldn't have to deal with any of this." She was so right and my heart went out to her. She was being forced to deal with something that was unorthodox for someone her age. This is was not the norm for a child, and she was wise enough to not only understand that but verbalized it.

We even make promises to ourselves, and when we will don't see it come to pass we begin to question and evaluate our lives. In my youth, I had grand plans for myself and my future. When I turned 30 years old, I remember evaluating my life, wondering what happened to the little girl who said, "This will never happen to me." Well at 30 years old, I realize that not only did it happen to me, but I had become complacent in it. There was a sudden rush that came over me to prove to myself that I was still that young girl filled with spirit and passion. Throughout my entire life, I always heard adults say that they had all these wonderful dreams but had to put them on hold because of life's moments. And not only did they put it on hold, but they completely dropped their dreams altogether. It is so frightened to hear adults reminisce about what they could have been, or had, but failed to fulfill and then look at your life and see that same pattern. You wonder if you have the passion, drive, or faith to fulfill your dream. After all, you promised yourself in your youth that you would not become what you had seen your entire life "a broken promise".

I knew the importance of a *promise keeper* early in my life. Each night as my father would leave for work I would ask him to bring me something home. If my father said that he would, believe me it would be like Christmas the next day as I waited with excitement until the next morning. And each time I would jump off my bunk bed, run in the living room and there it was my special gift on the dining room table. The gifts were awesome, but the fact that I could count on him to do what he said was the true *gift*. Those who have repeatedly suffered from broken promises from family and friends create open wounds and doors for rejection and often suffer with trust issues.

The spirit of rejection is worn like a coat covering the shoulders, the back and all sides. They experience the feeling of not being received or accepted. A person, who has a spirit of rejection, will cut off any opportunities in advance just to avoid expected rejection. They pad themselves with statements like, "I didn't want it anyway." "I wasn't ready anyway" or "I don't care anyway". These are defense statements, used to cope with rejection. The spirit of rejection is coupled with bitterness. Often you will see a rejected individual always scoping and expecting things to go wrong. They rarely cheer for someone else, because that only make them feel worst about their own situation. These feelings are not intentional, but have been fed and nurtured in the individual. A broken promise creates a lack of trust and enhances unpredictable feelings. Promises must be kept in order to build trust, comfort, stability and security.

My word is my bond is a phrase often used to express the dependability of someone's word. It simply means, I will always do what I promise to do. We have heard of the children's story about the little shepherd boy who cried wolf. He consistently lied about a wolf attacking his lambs, warning and crying out for the villagers to help. After playing this trick several times, when a wolf actually did show up, no one would respond or listen, and the little shepherd boy lost all of his lambs. The little shepherd boy credibility was tarnished, he was not reliable. Because of his character being flawed, he lost what he was supposed to protect. Although broken promises, are often minimized and overlooked the impact can definitely shape your life and those around you.

Understand how broken promises have affected your life. Forgive those who have hurt you by not following through with a promise. Their intentions were not necessarily to hurt or betray your trust. You have to release yourself from the spirit of rejection. It will continue to cover you and navigate your emotions unless you release it. Forgiveness is a decision to let go of resentment and thoughts of revenge. Forgiveness can even lead to feelings of understanding, empathy, and compassion for the one who has hurt you. Forgiveness doesn't mean that you deny the other person's responsibility for hurting you, and it doesn't minimize or justify the wrong. You can forgive the person without excusing the act. Forgiveness brings a kind of peace that helps you go on with your life. According to the Mayo Clinic Newsletter, Forgiveness can lead to:

- Healthier relationships
- Greater spiritual and psychological well-being
- Less anxiety, stress, and hostility
- Lower blood pressure
- Fewer symptoms of depression
- Stronger immune system
- Improved heart health
- Higher self-esteem

Repeat this release from the hold Broken Promises:

I have been hurt and scorned from broken promises, but I am no longer bound by that hurt. I forgive those who have disappointed me and have pushed me into the place that I have found myself in. I forgive myself for any and all missed assignments. I am free to be happy, loved, and empowered. I'm not under any curses that might have been brought on by opened doors created from brokenness. I resist the spirit of rejection, bitterness, and doubt. Greater things are coming to me and I'm anticipating the flow of positivity in abundance. I'm free to receive all of the great things that are in store for me. I will complete my assignments, and fulfill my purpose. Freedom is mine.

Chapter 4:
Legal Rights

Spiritual and Natural legal rights as a citizen guarantees the resident of a kingdom enjoys privileges and opportunities which the Kingdom offers. Luke 12:31 (ESV) states: *But rather seek ye the Kingdom of God; and all these things shall be added unto you.* What are you seeking? What are you expecting? We have a right to health, peace, life and prosperity. Often these rights are hindered due to a forfeit. When you entertain and shelter unhealthy thoughts and behavior, you forfeit your rights to peace of mind. Just like in the natural we have a right to be free and live in our homes. We have rights as U.S. citizens to vote, apply for federal employment and express ourselves. But if you commit a crime and is prosecuted and found guilty, you are no longer allowed to live in your home, vote, or even express yourself. Your freedom has been forfeited, and you are now in the custody of your local state authorities. Once you are incarcerated, you are told when to wake up, eat, exercise, and sleep. If you harbor poisonous behavior and thoughts, you will open doors of anger and strife. That's right you will become incarcerated by spirits directing your every move. For example, have you ever been happy, laughing and enjoying yourself and then all of a sudden a feeling comes over you of sadness. You start remembering all the things that are wrong in your life. And you feel as if you don't have a right to be happy. These thoughts should be cast down immediately and never entertained.

In October 2012, I planned my annual Harvest Fest for my family. I was so excited, because we had just moved and was celebrating our new home. My husband was at the store picking up last minute items while I picked up the kids after work. I hadn't heard from husband all day and began calling his cell phone. I became extremely nervous when he failed to answer after several attempts. Finally, a police officer answered the phone and informed me that my husband was having a seizure in the store and paramedics were on the scene. "Not my husband, he has never had a seizure", was my reply. The officer verified that it was my husband, and I was stunned. From that moment, my life completely changed. I met my husband at the hospital and was grateful that he was okay, but couldn't shake the thought of how and why, this happen. My husband had never been diagnosed or ever had a seizure during our 15yrs of marriage. I dissected every moment leading up to his seizure and after. It became my burden that I carried. My husband eventually healed and returned to himself. But I was a different woman. During this time, I begin to feel extremely vulnerable. What if something happens to my husband, what would I do? What if he has a seizure while driving? What if he has a seizure with me or the kids, what should I do? Will he be the same person, will I be the same? These thoughts held me captive. The store that my husband had his seizure in, became a vile place for me. I would literally get sick symptoms just going to the store. And my husband had no problem going and coming with no restrictions. I had to step back and evaluate the situation. I was behaving as if I was the one who had the seizure. I had opened a door of fear and doubt and forfeited my rights. I didn't apply what I knew and believed about the situation and found myself in a whirl wind of frustration. Romans 8:28 states: *And we know that in all things God works for the good of those who love him, who have been called according to his purpose.* I know this scripture very well, but what a struggle it was to apply it during this season. The struggle was because I chose to entertain the thoughts of oppression.

I remember when I struggled with depression, I felt so isolated. I knew that if I allowed the enemy to isolate me, he could kill me. Slowly drifting into a deeper state of depression with tears in my eyes and no strength to pull myself out of bed, I struggled. This was the first time that I realize the power and strength of fear. FEAR is so very paralyzing. According to Wikipedia, *fear is a feeling induced by perceived danger or threat that occurs in certain types of organisms, which causes a change in metabolic and organ functions and ultimately a change in behavior, such as fleeing, hiding, or freezing from perceived traumatic events. Fear in human beings may occur in response to a specific stimulus occurring in the present, or in anticipation or expectation of a future threat perceived as a risk to body or life. The fear response arises from the perception of danger leading to a confrontation with or escape from/avoiding the threat (also known as the fight-or-flight response), which in extreme cases of fear (horror and terror) can be a freeze response or paralysis.*

Fear is coupled with anxiety. Although fear can come on noticeably quickly, anxiety is very sneaky. These were some of the toughest years of my life; that's right years. Between loosing loved ones, having terminally ill family members, and my husband's sudden sickness and other family matters, I allowed my emotions to get the best of me and left the door right open. I felt overwhelmed and sorry for myself. Later I learned that several generations of my family members had experienced bouts of depression, anxiety, and fear. Initially, it brought me comfort to know that I wasn't the only person to have had these experiences, but then I realize that something deeper was happening. 1 John 4:18 (NIV) - *There is no fear in love; but perfect love casteth out fear: because fear hath torment. He that feareth is not made perfect in love.*

Fear prepares us to react to danger. Once we sense a potential danger, our body releases hormones that slow or shut down functions not needed for survival (such as our digestive system) and sharpen functions that might help us survive (such as eyesight). Our heart rate increases, and blood flows to muscles so we can run faster (anxiety). Our body also increases the flow of hormones to an area of the brain known as the *amygdala* to help us focus on the presenting danger and store it in our memory. The *amygdala* is an almond shaped mass of nuclei (mass of cells) located deep within the temporal lobes of the brain. There are two amygdalae, one situated in each brain hemisphere. The amygdala is a limbic system structure that is involved in many of our emotions and motivations, particularly those that are related to survival. It is involved in the processing of emotions such as fear, anger, and pleasure. The amygdala is also responsible for determining what memories are stored and where the memories are stored in the brain. Anxiety and panic attacks occur when environmental or emotional stressors convince your amygdala that you are in danger.

According to the calmclinic.com, the amygdala's direct and indirect effects on the body are listed and described below:

- **Catalyst:** First there is usually an emotional or environmental trigger: obsessive negative thoughts, or something you see, smell, hear, taste, or feel. Note that the trigger can also be inside you. You may not always know exactly what's triggering it. The subconscious mind is a very real thing.

- **Amygdala Reacts:** The amygdala reacts to the catalyst by preparing you to fight or run away. Triggers that are related to past emotional experiences produce stronger reactions in the amygdala, which (along with being responsible for fight or flight) is also believed to regulate long-term memory storage based on the strength of the emotions associated with a remembered event.

- **Adrenal Action**: Preparation for fight or flight involves the release of the adrenal chemical epinephrine into the bloodstream. Epinephrine is associated with adrenaline, and makes all your bodily processes speed up.

- **Blood Sugar**: The epinephrine released also has the side effect of raising blood sugar levels in the body. The blood sugar is then available to the muscles and can be converted into quick energy.

- **Shaking:** Shaking encourages blood to reach the extremities and can also be the result of the extra energy in the body.

- **Pounding Heart:** Epinephrine boosts the heart rate, which sends extra blood to power the body.

- **Flushing Extra blood** from the heart that the muscles don't use shows up as a red tinge in the face, neck, arms and/or chest.

- **Faster Breathing Rate** As your heart rate climbs, your lungs have to work faster to make sure the blood circulating in the body is supplied with enough oxygen.

- **Aching Chest**: Your lungs and heart working harder than normal can cause your chest to ache.

Calmclinic.com advises that he amygdala is not a *"thinking"* part of your brain so much as it is a *"reacting"* part. Its role is not to figure out why you are afraid, but to alert you if bad memories support a fight or flight reaction, and, if they do, to cause that fight or flight reaction to take place.

This explains why when you or a loved one has had a traumatic experience; the feelings can be triggered by a place, smell, or sound.

It can be difficult when your amygdala has already been triggered to "talk yourself out of" the reaction. From experience, I have tried to talk myself out of an anxiety attack with no success. There is no rationale in your thinking. The response is because other parts believe there is a danger.

It has been suggested that a possible way to "train" your amygdala is through a process called "fear exposure." The amygdala can't be trained through logical explanations or reasoning, and must instead be trained through simple repetition. Apply and practice speaking healing and restoration over your body and mind. Don't avoid your triggers but expose them.

Remember, I avoided going to certain stores because of what I felt when I went. I became handicap, avoiding any environment that would trigger my anxiety. I expected something to happen when I went out to the stores etc. I would look for the smallest sign and say "I'm having a bad day".

By repeatedly exposing yourself to the triggers or catalysts of your anxiety and thereby "teaching" the amygdala that in reality nothing bad occurs because of this exposure, it is possible for the amygdala to "learn" and (ideally) stop producing the fight of flight reaction in response to that particular trigger altogether. Avoidance was an enabler for me. In my mind, I was protecting myself by avoiding any environment that would take me back to the place of anxiety. Families fueled by anxiety tend to engage in avoidance behaviors. In other words, they don't take a ton of risks—even the healthy and developmentally appropriate ones.

I remember when I experienced an anxiety attack for the first time, I had been sick for a couple of weeks, but was pushing through how I felt. I had planned a wonderful day for me and my husband. We had breakfast date and was going to the movies and then for a brisk walk. We went to my favorite restaurant, and although I was still feeling ill, I was not going to let anything ruin our special day. As we sat in the movie theater, I was trying to self-medicate myself with no success. After going to the restroom several times, I sat down praying that this feeling would pass. All of a sudden as the symptoms progressed, I felt like something was really wrong. I felt like I was dreaming, my heart began to race, and my arms began to ache. Could I be having a heart attack or a stroke? My mind was racing out of control, and I could not believe this was happening to me. Will this happen here in a public movie theater? Will I collapse and have to be placed in an ambulance in front of all these people? As we left the movie theater, we went to the Emergency Room, and I was told by the doctor that the symptoms I was experiencing were anxiety. He said because of my pain and discomfort, I thought I was having a heart attack which triggered anxiety.

See I created the perfect formula for a perfect storm in my life. I had forfeited my rights to peace, joy and happiness by sheltering depression, anxiety and fear. Philippians 4:6-7 6 states: *Do not be anxious about anything, but in every situation, by prayer and petition, with thanksgiving, present your requests to God. And the peace of God, which transcends all understanding, will guard your hearts and your minds in Christ Jesus.* What an outstanding scripture. I found myself drawn to this scripture over and over again. It literally became my anthem to my new freedom. I even have this scripture decal on my kitchen wall to remind me every day what my responsibilities are. This scripture specifically deals with depression, anxiety and fear and the formula to remove it from your life forever.

First, it commands us not to be anxious about anything. The scripture doesn't list things to worry about and things not to worry about; it specifically states not to worry about anything. Instead of worrying, it tells us to take every situation in prayer and petition (a formal request to authority) with thanksgiving present them to God. Thanksgiving is significant because it's an act of faith that everything is already worked out. Imagine receiving a report from the doctor's office that your prognosis looks grim. Instead of crawling into a hole and throwing up both hands in defeat, imagine giving thanks as if your healing has already manifested as you make your request known. Oh, how that would completely confuse your enemies and even your doctor. To not just repeat the scripture but actually apply it and allow it to become a part of you as you become a part of it. I think that's why the bible is called the living word. It gives life and it is life. I believe that we were never supposed to just read it as if it was just words on paper, but we are to be the word and let it be in us.

Even though you can't see or feel it, there's a lot you can do to help keep that small, almond shaped bit of your brain in check when you find that it's working overtime. Taking care of your body and mind is the first step you should take. It's important to also sleep well, sleeping deeply for a healthy amount of time each day is crucial to maintaining a healthy state of mind and body. Also eating a regular and healthy diet is necessary to replenish your body when anxiety has sapped its resources.

Repeat this to establish authority and protect your rights:

By the authority given by my heavenly father, I cancel any and all contracts or deals made with my enemies directly or indirectly. All plans for my failure have been cancelled. I speak life, peace and happiness over my life and the lives of my seeds. I am not under in curse created by actions of any of my ancestors. I am free and delivered from all past transgressions. I do not forfeit any of our God-given rights. I claim my inheritance, and I will complete my assignments and fulfill my purpose.

Breaking Family Ties

Chapter 5:
Renewing Your Mind
(Power of Your Thoughts)

I remember sitting in a public place and enjoying the festivities when a man begins telling everyone within my area that he could smell natural gas. Now prior to him saying anything, I felt great with absolutely no symptoms, but as soon as he said that there is a gas leak, I began to panic. Not only did I panic but I began to physically feel ill, and weak. It was the strangest thing I had ever experienced. My legs were wobbly, and I felt light headed. I had watched the specials on home safety and read the articles, and clearly, I was experiencing exposure to natural gas. His words had an immediate reaction over me. Another gentleman came and eased all of our minds by verifying that everything was safe. There was never a gas leak, and we were never in any danger. I knew then if I could give myself physical symptoms based on untruth, how awesome would it be to use that same power for speaking life, prosperity and health over my life.

This is when I began the *"Renewed Mind Revolution"*. This movement states: We are born into a world of fear. As children, our parents established control by instilling fear. Don't go there or this will happen, don't do that or this will happen. Subconsciously these patterns have instilled a deep rooted fear into us. Throughout our lives we may wonder why we are hesitant to make decisions, fighting within ourselves seeking advice from others about decisions that we are more than capable of making on our own. This pattern created an inability of making simple decisions creating a doubt and lack of confidence. Renew Mind Revolution is a practice of untangling the pattern of doubt created by fear. This revolution is not yet widespread but will be soon. There is an awakening happening in our society which makes this the perfect timing for this reversal. The opportunities are there and waiting for revolutionaries. Revolutionaries who dare to think outside of the box and not be a status quo. This is a process to unravel what has been imparted from birth. Although we are our parent's child, we are not limited by their culture, tradition or character. We have a new character, we are a new creature designed to fulfill and execute our assignment.

Romans 12:2 (NIV) states: *Do not conform to the pattern of this world, but be transformed by the renewing of your mind. Then you will be able to test and approve what God's will is--his good, pleasing and perfect will.* Your thoughts are alive. According to Psychology Today dated 6/9/16 it has been estimated that we have anywhere from 25,000 to 50,000 thoughts a day.

Depression manifests in negative thinking before it creates a negative effect. One very successful way to combat depression is to understand how critical the quality of your thinking is to the maintaining and even intensifying your depression. Therefore the quickest way to change how you feel is to change how you think.

Positive and negative thinking are contagious.

"Men and women are not prisoners of fate, but only prisoners of their own minds. - Franklin D. Roosevelt. The thoughts that pass through your mind are responsible for everything that happens in your life. Your predominant thoughts influence your behavior and attitude and control your actions and reactions. As your thoughts are, so is your life. Proverbs 23:7 (KJV) reads for as he thinketh in his heart so is he: Eat and drink, saith he to thee; but his heart is not with thee. As a man thinks in his heart so is he, not what he speaks with his tongue. The thoughts of men's hearts do evidence what their spiritual state is. A man's inmost thinking is the true index to his character. You cannot know a man merely by listening to his words or watching his actions. There is always more, and often better, in men than comes into expression.

According to the Mayo Clinic researchers continue to explore the effects of positive thinking on health, health benefits that positive thinking may provide includes:

- Increased life span
- Lower rates of depression
- Lower levels of distress

- Greater resistance to the common cold
- Better psychological and physical well-being
- Reduced risk of death from cardiovascular disease
- Better coping skills during hardships and times of stress

Positive thinking enables you to cope with stressful situations reducing harmful health effects of stress on your body.

I remember a young lady that I met that suffered from chronic anxiety. She was unable to travel anywhere by herself and could not sit or stand in a crowd without someone assisting her. Her stress level was so high that she would begin crying from standing in a crowd alone. She would run out of public places when she felt overwhelmed. After speaking with her over time, I learned that she was married and had children. When her husband divorced her, she felt overwhelmed by the abandonment and the new responsibility of being a single mother. All of a sudden she had the sole responsibility of her children because her husband was no longer involved. I observed her talk herself right into a frenzy of madness. The more she reiterated her situation, the more she found herself stressed. We discussed her changing her perspective. It's so important to look at situations from different angles, and not become overwhelmed. If you are faced with only one option then, of course, you will feel swamped, but if you can see that there are other options and help then you can see a glimmer of hope.

Auto-pilot is term that I use to describe going through the motions and not living on purpose. Auto-pilot is a state of mind in which you wake up in the morning and immediately begin thinking about coming home and going back to bed. You participate in activities physically, but mentally you are far away. You enter the work office and immediately began thinking about when you are able to clock out. You are always waiting for something to come and change your current situation. You go through the motions every day until that moment arrives. I can't wait until I make more money, get a bigger house, get a better car, and finally get married. This is such a numbing existence, always existing but not living. Watching others explore and advance as you continue to wait. The wait is paralyzing and stressful. This experience is a detachment from reality. You're just traveling through to get to an end. Auto-pilot is an auto-cycle of life. You are not progressive in auto-pilot. You are always waiting on the edge. It is a numbing place of complacency. The time that you lose in auto-pilot is irreplaceable. It feels like you are placed in a glass box with a 360 degree view but the inability to touch, feel or participate.

Getting through the numbness of existing and not living requires the renewing of your mind. Take one day at a time. Time is something that you can't retrieve, so there is never a reason to waste time. We need to get rid of our sinful attitudes, our negative, critical ways of thinking, and our selfish thoughts. Be mindful of what you are feeding your soul, mind and spirit. If you are feeding your spirit man unhealthy and negative food, then you will have a negative and unhealthy mind. This includes the company that we entertain, the music we listen to, and the movies that we watch.

The biblical languages possess no one word parallel to the English definition of the mind. KJV translates at least six different Hebrew terms for the word mind. The primary word is *leb*, which means "heart." For example, Moses said, "The Lord hath sent me to do all these works; for I have not done them of mine own mind" (Numbers 16:28). The word *nephesh* (soul) is translated "mind" in Deuteronomy 18:6 when it refers to the desire of a man's mind (soul) and in Genesis 23:8 where it refers to mind in the sense of a decision or judgment. The word *ruach* (spirit) is rendered "mind" in Genesis 26:35. It speaks of the "grief of mind" (spirit) which Isaac and Rebekah experienced because Esau married heathen wives. Also used are the words *lebab* (heart) in Ezekiel 38:10; **yetser** (imagination) in Isaiah 26:3; and *peh* (mouth, speech) in Leviticus 24:12).

The more common terms for mind, however, are **nous** and *dianoia*. *Dianoia* occurs twelve times in the New Testament. It refers to "thinking through" or "thinking over" of something or to the "understanding" or "sentiment" which results from that process of reflection. *Nous* is the most prominent term for mind; it occurs twenty-four times.

Nous represents the "seat of understanding," the place of "knowing and reasoning." It also includes feeling and deciding. It sometimes includes the counsels and purposes of the mind. An example is Paul's statement: "Let every man be fully persuaded in his own mind" (Romans 14:5). Mind is sometimes associated with the human soul. Three times in the King James Version the word *psuche* (soul or life) is rendered by the word mind. Philippians 1:27 says believers are to be of "one mind (soul)."

Reprobate Mind phrase is only found once in the Bible, but there related phrases that occur several times:

"And even as they did not like to retain God in their knowledge, God gave them over to a reprobate mind, to do those things which are not convenient" (Romans 1:28) These people had gone so far in sin, "they did not like to retain God in their knowledge," and so God gave them what they wanted. They did not want God, righteousness, holiness, cleanness, or purity, so God "gave them over."

"Now as Jannes and Jambres withstood Moses, so do these also resist the truth: men of corrupt minds reprobate concerning the faith." (2 Timothy 3:8). Here the reprobation is regarding the resistance to the truth because of corrupt minds.

"They profess that they know God; but in works they deny him, being abominable, and disobedient, and unto every good work reprobate." (Titus 1:16) Therefore, the reprobate mind is one that is corrupt and worthless.

The Greek word translated "reprobate" in the New Testament is adokimos, which means literally "unapproved, that is, rejected; by implication, worthless (literally or morally)." Those who have reprobate minds live corrupt and selfish lives.

Have you rejected the truth and attempted to encourage others to denounce the existence of God and His son Jesus Christ? Have you rejected a life of righteousness, holiness, cleanness, and purity? Have chosen to live a life of sin and hatred despite knowing the wages of sin is death? Have you heard the word of God but yet still choose not to believe? Have you stated that you know God, but deny him amongst your peers and in public? Then you have a reprobated mind. And according to Romans 1:28, God will give you what you want, a life without His influence or presence. He will give you over to the life that you have chosen for yourself.

Chapter 6:
Complacency Is a Curse

Complacency is a feeling of being satisfied with how things are, and not wanting to try to make them better (Merriam Webster). Complacency is definitely a curse that I have seen throughout generations of families. Due to the repetitive nature of many of our behaviors, complacency is an ever-present danger. When a person becomes complacent his alertness level for the task decreases, and so does his performance. Our routine "kills us". Proverbs 1:32 (NIV) states: *For the waywardness of the simple will kill them, and the complacency of fools will destroy them.*

The only constant in life is change. Once you stop striving, once you stop learning, once you stop moving forward, that's when you begin to die. Until you are ready to die, do not become complacent. I know of families that live in the same town and never travel out of the community for anything. They live, shop, and socialize in their town. Whatever is trending in their community, such as clothes, hairstyles, music etc. is the norm only to those individuals in that community. This is all that they know, and they are comfortable in their comfort zone. This is where their grandparents lived, their parents grew up and now it's also where they call home. We are not talking tradition or culture. No, we are talking about the stagnation of three to four generations.

I remember as a child; fear was instilled into me about everything. I don't want to sound dramatic about it, but really just about everything. It's confusing to be told that the sky is the limit for you and that you can accomplish whatever you desire as long as you don't go here, don't go there, don't do this and don't ever do that. If you don't follow this strict path, expect hell and brimstone to fall on your head. Okay, it wasn't exactly verbalized like that, but it was implied. How painful is it to follow a faith of the impossible only to back yourself into a small corner, limiting your reach and your resources. What a struggle it was to have so much internal struggle as a youngster, wanting to please everyone around you, yet be true to yourself.

I didn't have any desires to be a copycat of anyone I wanted to be free to be whom I was created to be. My faith tells me in 2 Timothy 1:7 (NIV) states: *For the Spirit God gave us does not make us timid, but gives us power, love, and self-discipline.* Psalm 84:11(NIV) states: *For the LORD God is a sun and shield; the LORD bestows favor and honor; no good thing does he withhold from those whose walk is blameless.* I have always had very innocent faith and believed wholeheartedly what the bible said that I can have and who it said I could be. I've always believed in putting the word to the test. So as a youngster watching spiritual leaders practice *flip-flop faith* just about knocked me off my feet. See I was a great student, and one of my best qualities was listening and literally soaking up knowledge. You can't tell me to try one thing and then turn around and apply something else. Either I was going too completely with full force practice and apply this or walk away. I was so sick, physically and emotionally sick of going through the theatrics of faith. I could no longer stomach the traditionalism of just churching. Really, how long can you go to a service and go through the motions only to walk away feeling good but not being good. I had seen too many spiritual leaders fall, get sick, walk away or die pre-maturely. I looked around and realized the complacency was a curse. Just going through the motions and not digging deeper and seeking more is a curse. I did not want to read that all things were working out for my good, but not expect it, not walk, talk and speak like it was.

Epidemic complacency is described as lukewarm, unzealous or uncommitted. "I know your deeds—that you are neither cold nor hot...So, because you are lukewarm...I will spit you out of My mouth....Those whom I love I rebuke and discipline. So be zealous, and repent. He who overcomes, I will grant him the right to sit with Me on My throne, just as I overcame and sat down with my Father on His throne."(Revelation 3:15-21).

Everyone experiences complacency. It invades areas once occupied by our passion, interest, desire, and focus. When complacent, the valued things that had captivated our thoughts, hearts, and energies tend to fade from priority and can even become a boring routine of everyday life. Burnout in our work life, loss of fire in relationships, and the lack of zeal for things we once held important are common experiences. The shame is not in complacency but in the failure to recognize it and take corrective measures to rectify the situation. Complacency can creep into the life of the musician whose music, once an expression of the soul, is now just singing notes. It can impact the physician, the mechanic, the cook, and the preacher. The effects of complacency are much more serious than half-cooked food or warmed-over sermons. Our complacency kills the environment; it ruins our health, and it steals away our days, months, and years. Like a curse, complacency sometimes descends upon us unaware. The recognition of how complacency moves in and impacts our life is important.

Proverbs 18:21 states: *The tongue has the power of life and death, and those who love it will eat its fruit.* I've seen this scripture used to instill the fear I described earlier as if it only said the tongue has the power of death. But the scriptures states, power of life and death. That's right LIFE that same tongue that you use to keep you in the place of stagnation, can SHIFT you into a place of liberation. The power referred to here is not the physical power of the tongue as a muscle, but the power of the words it produces. The word "tongue" was not used in relation to God Himself. It's a word used of human speech. So we can see that the Word of God is saying that our speech is tremendously important, powerful and significant. It is a matter of life and death. There are three primary factors that encourage the physical side of complacency. They are:

- Fatigue
- Too many things happening simultaneously
- Too few things happening
- Inertia-The tendency of objects to keep moving in a straight line at constant velocity.
- Resistance to Change

Complacency encourages the absolute minimum. It's easy to be average and to settle.

Repeat this to break the chains of complacency:

Complacency and stagnation are no longer welcomed in my life. I am focused and purpose driven. I will no longer operate in fear to expand and explore. I am not bound by any curses and I declare my freedom to complete my assignment in excellence. I will no longer put off what I should be doing right now. I know that I am forgiven and loved. I will pursue my purpose with passion. Today is a new day and a new beginning.

Breaking Family Ties

Chapter 7:
Proclamation

Merriam-Webster dictionary describes Proclamation as the act of saying something in a public, official, or definite way. The act of proclaiming something is an official statement or announcement made by a person in power or by a government.

2 Corinthians 4:13 (NIV) - *We having the same spirit of faith, according as it is written, I believed, and therefore have I spoken; we also believe, and therefore speak.* Regardless of your current situation or dilemma you have to speak and apply what you believe. Luke 6:43-45 reads, *"No good tree bears bad fruit, nor does a bad tree bear good fruit. Each tree is recognized by its own fruit. People do not pick figs from thorn bushes, or grapes from briers. A good man brings good things out of the good stored up in his heart, and an evil man brings evil things out of the evil stored up in his heart. For the mouth speaks what the heart is full of.*

James 3:11 writes *Can both fresh water and salt water flow from the same spring*? Have you ever heard a person contradict themselves all in one breath? "I'm broke and don't have any money, but God is a provider". "I'm sick, but

I'm feeling better". It seems so innocent right? I mean after all, they concluded the statement with God is a provider. But they already declared that they are broke. It is so easy to speak negative, because of our culture and environment. When you see someone who has been sick for a while, they first thing they do is catch you up on what they have been going through. They want to relay to you their struggle. I remember this young lady who would always say that "today is a bad day" to relay her struggle. Now you may be thinking that it is not wrong with sharing your tough moments, after all, we need the support from each other. There is absolutely nothing wrong with sharing your moments; it is actually healthy to share our journey. But remember we have to mindful of how we speak because there is power in our thinking and proclaiming. So how do we speak on something that we don't see or feel? If I am broke, with no funds, how do say I'm rich. If I'm sick, and broken how do I say I'm healed and complete? Luke 6:45 states: *A good man brings good things out of the good stored up in his heart, and an evil man brings evil things out of the evil stored up in his heart. For the mouth speaks what the heart is full of.* Speak what your heart desires the most. The truth is that every word you speak has power to build or destroy, to restore or cause loss, to heal or break the spirit, to bring delight or despair, to bless or curse.

Stop lining up your words with death, lack, poverty, despair, sickness, and curses. Instead speak life, joy, peace, prosperity and health over your life and your heirs. James

3:3-6 9 (NIV) states it best by writing: *When we put bits into the mouths of horses to make them obey us, we can turn the whole animal. Or take ships as an example. Although they are so large and are driven by strong winds, they are steered by a very small rudder wherever the pilot wants to go. Likewise, the tongue is a small part of the body, but it makes great boasts. Consider what a great forest is set on fire by a small spark. The tongue also is a fire, a world of evil among the parts of the body. It corrupts the whole body, sets the whole course of one's life on fire, and is itself set on fire by hell.* What a profound scripture. James is educating the reader on the power of words. He gives a great analogy on not only the size of the tongue but the power of its application.

Verse 12 states: *My brothers and sisters, can a fig tree bear olives, or a grapevine bear figs? Neither can a salt spring produce fresh* water. We can't play on both teams. If you are watching a baseball game, you are never rooting for both teams. You are wearing sports gear for only one team. You would never wear both team spirit gears at the same time. No one says I will cheer for Team A during the first half and Team B during the second half.

So many are torn between doing what they are accustomed and what they believe. When we know better, we do better. We don't compromise, or try to please everybody. Speak life, and you will get joy, compassion, love, and kindness. Speak brokenness and death, and that is exactly what you will get.

Repeat this Proclamation:

With authority given to me by the Spirit of God, I declare I am healed. I'm not broken, but I am complete. I'm not angry or bitter, but I have peace and joy. I'm not living in lack, but all my needs are provided. I don't want for anything. My heart is full, and mind is at ease. I forgive those who have hurt me, and I am forgiven. I'm walking, talking and breathing liberty. Freedom is a God given right, and I proclaim it over my life and my heirs. I will complete my assignments and fulfill my purpose.

Chapter 8:
Purpose Filled Life

Today we live in a society where the value of life has diminished. Reports of the death toll rising saturates the news coverage. Mothers and fathers are in despair due to the untimely death of their children. Children are running rapid in the streets with weapons holding communities hostage. Fathers are murdering entire families because of economic pressure. People are walking into churches, synagogues, and temples opening up in gun fire taking lives as they worship. Movie theaters, restaurants and concerts halls are filled with gun fire leaving people in pain, fear and despair. Schools are practicing lock down scenarios to better prepare children in the case of terrorism or loose gun men. Children are unable to play in parks or front yards without bullets flying over their heads putting their precious lives at risk. With death all around it is easy to lose focus on purpose. The purpose at this point becomes surviving to see another day. This generation takes the motto: "I will take you out, before you take me out". A life without purpose is an automatic death sentence. When a person has no concern for their life, they will not have concern for your life.

Purpose is the reason why something is done or used, the aim or intention of something. The feeling of being determined to do or achieve something. The aim or goal of a person; what a person is trying to do, become, etc. (Merriam-Webster). Your purpose in life should not be getting up and just existing in auto-pilot. The concerns of this world and the needs of your family can drift you away from your true purpose. The definition of purpose is what a person is trying to do or become. What are you trying to become?

Without hope, a feeling of expectation and desire for a certain thing to happen it is impossible to understand your purpose. Jeremiah 29:11 (NIV) writes: *For I know the plans I have for you, declares the LORD, plans for welfare and not for evil, to give you a future and a hope.* Despite what you see, what you feel, what you think you know, there is HOPE. 2 Corinthians 4:16-18 (NIV) encourages us not to lose hope: *So we do not lose heart. Though our outer self is wasting away, our inner self is being renewed day by day. For this light momentary affliction is preparing for us an eternal weight of glory beyond all comparison, as we look not to the things that are seen but to the things that are unseen. For the things that are seen are transient, but the things that are unseen are eternal.*

Shift your focus! Easily said than done you might say. But the alternative is wandering lost and confused with the surety of an unfulfilled life. According to 1 Corinthians 10:13 (NIV) *No temptation has overtaken you except what is common to mankind. And God is faithful; he will not let you be tempted beyond what you can bear. But when you are tempted, he will also provide a way out so that you can endure it.* We are equipped and designed to fulfill our purpose. Because we deal with life's moments, sometimes we can get off track, and the more we become distracted, the further off track we become. People caught in the cycle of generational poverty often are in survival mode. They are focused on whatever challenges greet them each day, whether that's paying the rent, buying food or taking care of a health problem. Have you ever known someone from your childhood and you see him years later, and wonder what has happened in their life. You know from first glance that they have had a difficult life. The struggle covers their entire presence. They don't even have to tell you anything; you already know that they are dealing with issues. They may have had grand plans for their future as a child, but life's moment has re-directed them from their purpose filled life.

A life without a purpose is a life without a destination. Purpose filled life is deeper than a career choice. Finding a purpose is ultimately a spiritual endeavor because it involves a process of connecting with something greater than yourself. Purpose always works its way out in action because passion is, at root, a matter of desire.

All things start in the mind. The great cathedrals and mosques of the world, the pyramids, the modern world, cars, planes and space ships all the wonders of the ancient and the modern worlds they all started as ideas, dreams.

Breaking Family Ties

Chapter 9:
The Buck Stops Here

The Buck Stops Here is simply saying the responsibility is not passing beyond this point. Taking responsibility for what others has passed on. We discussed the negative traits we can inherit from generation to generation. Even behavior and social behavior can be passed on. But the buck stops here. For the sake of me and my children, the curse ends now.

Abraham was an obedient "friend of God" (James 2:23). He rejected the pagan culture of his family line and chose to live a new and positive way of life. At God's request Abraham left that environment and even his own family to follow the course God set before him. In doing so, he would become known as "the father of the faithful." What a trailblazer Abraham was, for rejecting what was the norm for his family line and choosing a new and positive way of life. By taking ownership, he took responsibility and therefore blessed his family line for generations.

Family is the foundation of our society. Family is considered a group consisting of parents and children living together in a household. Family is also the descendants of a common ancestor. Family is our first lesson in creating relationships. We learn from our family how to communicate and socialize. We learn about ourselves by the interactions with our family. Families are crucial partners in promoting positive social skills. But there are negative and unhealthy traits and skills that we can indirectly adopt from our family. Although you may have deep rooted personal issues that stem from generational conditions, does not mean that you are destined to continue the pattern.

In 1974 American singer and songwriter Harry Chapin recorded a song titled "Cat's in the Cradle." The song is about a father who is too busy to spend time with his son, instead offering false promises to spend time with him in the future.

Over time, the boy grows up to become a man very much like his father, focused on career and other personal pursuits at the expense of time with his son. As the father grows old and finally has time to look back on his life, he deeply desires time with his son and has a meaningful relationship with him. Sadly, the father comes to realize that his son has adopted the same materialistic priorities he had, and so a close relationship will never happen. The last verse concludes with this sad line: "And as I hung up the phone it occurred to me, he'd grown up just like me—my boy was just like me."

People can be very selfish and live a life uncaring to the effects on their children, and their children to come. Long term effects by the actions of parents and grandparents are real. The Scriptures often remind us that it's important to think generationally. Exodus 34:7, "Keeping mercy for thousands, forgiving iniquity and transgression and sin, and that will by no means clear the guilty; visiting (punishing) the iniquity of the fathers upon the children, and upon the children's children, unto the third and to the fourth generation". Curses are the result of breaking God's law, and many sins are perpetuated in the next generation by the poor example of the previous generation. Strengths and weaknesses within an individual family culture are the results of its environment or choices. This includes values, priorities, and decision-making skills. When negative choices and a bad home environment become deeply entrenched within a family culture, individual members can become self-destructive and unknowingly pass on these traits.

I remember a young man that based upon his family history adopted a self-destructive behavior. He was raised in a family with alcohol and drugs. For the first 10 years of his life, he would boast about his innocence and joy of childhood. But once his mother and father began the abuse of drugs the dynamic of his life was forever changed. Jumping from house to house and even being homeless as a teenager, he struggled to change his life. But no matter what he did or where he went, he always found himself making self-destructive choices. Whenever things were going pretty smooth in his life, he would shift gears and make an outlandish move. It was as if he was being drawn into a pit each time he attempted to crawl out. Unfortunately, I have heard this type of story from many over the years. A very successful man loses his family and career because he is still carrying the pain of his youth. A woman walking away from her children, because when she sees them, she sees her own pain from her youth and can't cope. I've seen a 60 year old woman cry over the verbal abuse of her mother that she experience as a child. There is no doubt that childhood experiences can affect your life as an adult. These are deep rooted issues that must be addressed. The worst mistake that you can make is pretending as if it has never happened. You can't cover a bullet wound with a band aide. Don't underestimate your experiences by down playing them as if they have no bearing on your future. Stop accepting the past mistakes as your destined prison cell. Just because Uncle Jack was an alcoholic but the life of the party does not mean that you have to take his place. Uncle Jack didn't do anything with his life but throw it away in a bottle. Don't tell me that your mother raise 12 kids with no husband and no money, so if she can do it so can you. Your mother struggle her entire life, and never wanted the same for her children. She took you to school and church praying that you would do better with your life. So why are you embracing a life she never intended for you to have. You saw your father angry everyday stressed trying to take care of the family and died young overworked and underpaid. Don't walk in his footsteps, saying that's the only way you know. A life filled with purpose and no executions is a travesty. Your mother allowed men to abuse her and use her body as if she was their property. Don't repeat this cycle of abuse. You deserve to be loved and cared for by someone who love and treasures you. Your father raised his hand to you in anger and struck you. Don't look in the face of your son/daughter and take their innocence by repeating the cycle. Don't look away when your sons and daughters are smoking and doing drugs saying they only get to be young once and besides you did it at their age. Your father disrespected your mother and was unfaithful pulling the family apart. Don't repeat his cycle saying, "Like father like son".

Make a decision that you won't wait for a change, but you will be the change. You don't have to look for some drastic event to shake up and change the patterns set before you, but you can be the SHIFT. No more poverty, no more pain, no more abuse, no more hurt but Freedom. Learn to forgive those family members who have caused you pain. You do not have to agree with what they are doing, but do not carry hate in your heart for them. Unforgiveness will take you to a place of bitterness, and this is never a place where you want to be. Also remember to forgive yourself.

Be victorious, not a victim. A victim is one that has suffered harm or who is tricked or swindled. Victory is overcoming an enemy or success in a struggle. Victorious is having won a victory. You are victorious, despite what you are thinking right now; know that you are already victorious. This book didn't reach your hands by accident. It was a strategic plan by God to assure that you rightly informed to be spiritually enlightened and free. 2 Corinthians 2:14 states: "Now thanks be to God who always leads us in triumph in Christ." Life is full of transition, changes, and challenges but God is able. Religion is not reliable, but relationship makes the difference."

In the Bible, Joseph's vision and purpose was bigger than Potiphar's house. Even in the prison, the warden puts Joseph in charge of the other prisoners. He came in contact with Pharaoh's chief cupbearer and the chief baker in prison. The Bible tells us that they both had dreams that Joseph interpret. Joseph said in three days the chief cupbearer would be reinstated, but the chief baker would be hanged. When it came to pass, he requested that the cupbearer to mention him to Pharaoh and secure his release from prison. The cup bearer was reinstalled in office forget to mention Joseph. Joseph spent two more years in prison before the cupbearer remembered Joseph and spoke of his skills to interpret Pharaoh's dreams. Seven years of abundance followed by Seven years of famine. Joseph advised Pharaoh to store surplus grain during years of abundance. Pharaoh released him and put him in charge of all of the land of Egypt. Pharaoh took his Signet ring and put it on Joseph's hand, then clothed him in fine linen and put a gold necklace around his neck. Joseph was very successful and had the opportunity of reuniting with his brothers and father.

Pharaoh had such a high regard for Joseph practically making him his equal. At the age of seventeen, Joseph had a dream, before the age of thirty the dream was fulfilled. A victorious mind doesn't mean that adversity won't come, but it will not have the means of conquering.

2 Corinthians 4:8-10 states: We are hard pressed on every side, but not crushed; perplexed, but not in despair; persecuted, but not abandoned; struck down, but not destroyed. We always carry around in our body the death of Jesus, so that the life of Jesus may also be revealed in our body. You are never alone, not abandoned, not an orphan, not destroyed, not a victim but VICTORIOUS!

Love your family, even those who have hurt you. This easily said than done but it is important for your advancement. I think a healthy and effective approach is to see them as victims as well. They may not necessarily understand their impact on your life and was only repeating what was done to them. This is no way an excuse or a pass but reality. Remember what it was like for you, before your eyes were opened. I call this experience a spiritual enlightenment. Let's look at the life of Paul. Paul was known as the persecutor of all Christians until he had a transforming vision. Five years after the crucifixion of Jesus Christ, Paul was perhaps 30 years old and on his way to Damascus, when he encountered a light from heaven and the voice of God. Paul described it as "God was pleased to reveal his son to me, in order that I might preach him among gentiles." Through Paul's experience, Paul understood what it was like to think that you are serving God and carrying out his plans only for God to reveal that you are not. This heavenly vision showed Paul that the very God hole he had been serving, he had radically misunderstood. For Paul the impossible became real. He spent three days praying in darkness and fasting. Cut-off from his past, Paul had to come to his senses before his vision was restored. The eyes of his heart had been when enlightened. Paul was a highly trained and Jew, and his understanding of the law, tradition, Israel's history and God's grace and love had to be completely rethought.

We are often contaminated by our traditions, rituals, and religious ceremonies. We need to be decontaminated and the focus on the will of God. God called Paul out, not to simply repeat the words of others, but to dig deeply into the revelation that he himself had received. So fulfilling his charge, he prays for spiritual understanding. He wants the believer to see clearly and really understand who Christ is and all He has done for us.

My transforming moment occurred at the age of 22yrs old. I had just gotten married and given birth to our first son in December. By the month of February I was very ill, and hospitalized. While lying in my hospital bed, I was approached by my sister, brother and husband. They had come to tell me that as I sat in my hospital bed, my father had just died in his hospital bed, a couple of floors above my room. Immediately I felt smothered and crushed. Everything that matters to me was questioned. What I thought I knew, I didn't know. What I thought I wanted no longer matter. Who was I and where was I going. God took a hold of me that day, just like Paul on the road to Damascus. I had experienced a spiritual enlightening that would change my life forever. Don't be afraid to allow yourself to be transformed and released from conformity. John 10:10 states: The thief comes only to steal and kill and destroy; I have come that they may have life and have it to the full.

Breaking Family Ties

Chapter 10:
Freedom

It is for freedom that Christ has set us free. Stand firm, then, and do not let yourselves be burdened again by a yoke of slavery (Galatians 5:1). The metaphor is taken from oxen put under a yoke, and implicated with it, from which they cannot disengage themselves.

A yoke is a heavy wooden harness that fits unto one or more oxen. It is attached to a piece of equipment the oxen are to pull. There are two types of yokes: a bow yoke and a head yoke.

A bow yoke is a shaped wooden crosspiece bound to the necks of a pair of oxen or sometimes horses. It is held on the animal's neck by an oxbow, usually u-shaped, that transmits force from the animal's shoulders.

A head yoke is a yoke which fits onto the head of the oxen and has carved out sections which the horns fit into. The yoke is strapped to the head of the oxen with yoke straps and ox pads. The yoke is held on to not rest on their necks.

Oxen are yoked together to serve a purpose. In the New Testament, the yoke is described as a partnership with Jesus Christ, which implies that He carries our load, our burdens, etc. Christ's yoke is not easy to the self-willed. Like an unweaned child, they are continually chaffing (hot, rubbing and irritated) in their bondage but as of Christ's yoke is Iron (heavy on the neck), and does not chafe. Take my yoke upon you and learn from me, for I am gentle and humble in heart, and you will find rest for your souls (Matt 11:29). What or Who are you yoked with? Our life's choices can make our journey more difficult than it has to be. Have you ever heard the saying "You made your bed, so now lay in it". This phrase is implying that your actions, has made your life uncomfortable or troublesome, so now you have to deal with it. But you are designed and predestined to live a life of liberty.

He gave freedom to man but cannot hold anyone "free," so long as his own conscience locks him up into the fear of death and punishment. The mind which has places which it is afraid to touch can never expatiate (atone) everywhere; and the mind which cannot go anywhere, never is "free." It is the sense of pardon which is that man's emancipation. So if the Son sets you free, you will be free indeed (John 8:36). This is not a sensational sense of freedom, but it is as deep rooted as your issues. It is your God given birthright to be truly free. Let us stop blaming our environment. Let us alter it, or use it, or leave it, without complaining, but with sympathy, basing our actions on love. That's right, stop wasting time complaining and wallowing in your issues and change them. Change them by acknowledging, accepting, forgiving, loving and letting go.

Acknowledge what has happened in your family and how it has impacted your life and vow to end it for the sake of yourself and your children. Accept and declare that this is not the plan for your life or your seed. Forgive those who have hurt you indirectly and directly. Love your family and pray for their healing in the areas that has impacted the family cycle. Let go of the pain and anger. Resist the desire for retaliation and mockery of those who have negatively impacted your life.

Freedom is not an unattainable gift, but it is right within your reach. Don't allow the false illusion of depth keep you from reaching out and accepting your right to a brand new beginning. You deserve a fresh start and a new beginning. Despite the past mistakes and failure of the family tree, you have a right to good health, life, liberty and the pursuit of happiness better known as freedom. Not only free in the natural, but spiritually free as well. Be free to dream, believe and achieve. Don't live a life expecting the worse or accepting mediocrity when you know that you are able to achieve more. Don't limit yourself by backing yourself into a corner.

But they that wait upon the Lord shall renew their strength; they shall mount up with wings as eagles; they shall run, and not be weary; and they shall walk, and not faint (Isa 40:31).

Eagles have long, broad wings and tails which easily support their weight when flying, and can glide long distances by holding their wings out stiffly, catching the air currents and updrafts, enabling them to soar high into the sky, far higher than other birds. There are four basic mechanics to the eagle flight.

The first is lift. Lift force is created by the action of airflow on the wing, which is known as an airfoil. The lift force occurs because the air pressure is higher below the wing and lower above the wing. Just as an eagle, you must position yourself for take-off. You are pressure on every side, and it is time for a change, time to shift.

The second mechanic is gliding. Eagles obtain a mixture of forward and vertical force from their wings. This is due to the lift force being generated at a right angle. Once you have embraced the need to shift, you will take off finding that you are equipped to handle this. The shift will be an unfamiliar territory but a necessary change.

One of the fundamental mechanics of bird flight is flapping. When a bird flaps, its wings continue to create lift. This constant lift is rotated forward to create thrust that counteracts drag and increases speed. The two stages of flapping are the down stroke, which provides most of the thrust, and the up stroke. You have dedicated yourself to the change, even though it is a frightening experience for you with ups and downs, it will begin to get better over time. Perseverance is the key.

The final mechanic in bird flight is drag. The three major drag forces that impede upon a bird's flight are frictional, form and lift-induced drag. Once you have kept course and applied all that you have learned, you will begin to see and feel the impact and flight of freedom. You and others around you will see the beauty of your flight. It has been a challenging course to get here, but now you are free. Expand your wings and soar.

Breaking Family Ties